Developing Nu~~mber~~

HANDLING DATA

ACTIVITIES FOR THE DAILY MATHS LESSON

year

5

Hilary Koll and Steve Mills

A & C BLACK

Contents

Line graphs

Databases

Handling data project

Resources

Answers

Reprinted 2003

Published 2002 by A & C Black Publishers Limited
37 Soho Square, London W1D 3QZ
www.acblack.com

ISBN 0-7136-6299-9

Copyright text © Hilary Koll and Steve Mills, 2002
Copyright illustrations © Kirsty Wilson, 2002
Copyright cover illustration © Charlotte Hard, 2002
Editors: Lynne Williamson and Marie Lister

The authors and publishers would like to thank Jane McNeill and Corinne McCrum for their advice in producing this series of books.

A CIP catalogue record for this book is available from the British Library.

Printed in Great Britain by St Edmundsbury Press Ltd, Bury St Edmunds, Suffolk.

A & C Black uses paper produced with elemental chlorine-free pulp, harvested from managed sustainable forests.

Introduction

Developing Numeracy: Handling Data is a series of four photocopiable activity books for Key Stage 2, designed to be used during the daily maths lesson. It focuses on the fifth strand of the National Numeracy Strategy *Framework for teaching mathematics*. The activities are intended to be used in the time allocated to pupil activities; they aim to reinforce the knowledge and develop the facts, skills and understanding explored during the main part of the lesson. They provide practice and consolidation of the objectives contained in the framework document.

Year 5 supports the teaching of mathematics by providing a series of activities which develop essential skills in collecting, representing and interpreting numerical data. On the whole the activities are designed for children to work on independently, although this is not always possible and occasionally some children may need support.

Year 5 encourages children to:
- use the language associated with probability to discuss events, including those with equally likely outcomes. Discuss the chance or likelihood of particular events;
- solve a problem by collecting, organising, representing, extracting and interpreting data in tables, graphs and charts, including those generated by a computer, for example bar charts, bar line charts and line graphs;
- make a simple database;
- find the mode of a set of data.

Extension

Many of the activity sheets end with a challenge (**Now try this!**) which reinforces and extends the children's learning, and provides the teacher with the opportunity for assessment. The instructions are clearly presented so that children can work independently. On occasion, you may wish to read out the instructions and explain the activity before children begin working on it. For some of the challenges, the children will need to record their answers on a separate piece of paper. Sometimes the activity will require children to represent data in the form of a graph or chart and squared paper (or alternatively a computer with a handling data package) may be necessary.

Differentiated activities

Some of the activity sheets within this book are differentiated. A less challenging activity is indicated by a rocket icon: and a more challenging activity is indicated by a shooting star icon: . These activity sheets could be given to different groups within the class, or all children could complete the first sheet and children requiring further extension could then be given the second sheet.

Organisation

Very little equipment is needed, but it will be useful to have available: rulers, sharp pencils, squared paper, scissors, coloured pencils, counters, dice and ICT handling data software packages. You will need to provide measuring equipment (metre sticks, tape measures or trundle wheels) for page 21. Blank probability scales, database, bar chart, and bar line chart/line graph are provided on pages 43 to 46.

The activities in this book could be incorporated into lessons for other curriculum subjects, for example history, ICT, geography or science. The National Numeracy Strategy recommends exploiting opportunities for drawing on mathematical experience within other primary subjects, and handling data is a topic rich in cross-curricula investigations.

To help teachers select appropriate learning experiences for the children, the activities are grouped into sections within this book. However, the activities do not have to be used in that order unless otherwise stated. The sheets are intended to support, rather than direct, the teacher's planning.

Some activities can be made easier or more challenging by masking or substituting some of the numbers. You may wish to reuse some pages by copying them onto card and laminating them, some others you might want to enlarge onto A3 paper.

ICT

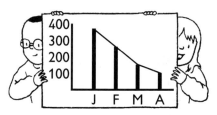

On most occasions where pupils are asked to represent data in a graphical or tabular form, a computer could be used for this purpose. Some programs allow more than one type of graph to be drawn, and comparisons of this type are very useful. Spreadsheets could be used to assist children in collecting information as part of a survey.

Where children are researching their own topics for handling data, safe Internet sites could be used. Acceptable sites can often be accessed through a local educational authority's website or through kid-safe searches as part of most search engines. Some websites are suggested on page 5.

Teachers' notes

Brief notes are provided at the foot of each page giving ideas and suggestions for maximising the effectiveness of the activity sheets. These can be masked before copying.

Whole-class warm-up activities

The following activities provide some practical ideas which can be used to introduce or reinforce the main teaching part of the lesson, or to provide an interesting basis for discussion.

Probability

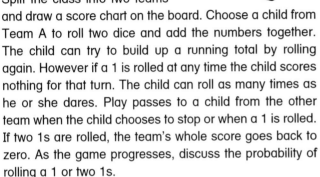

Risk

Split the class into two teams and draw a score chart on the board. Choose a child from Team A to roll two dice and add the numbers together. The child can try to build up a running total by rolling again. However if a 1 is rolled at any time the child scores nothing for that turn. The child can roll as many times as he or she dares. Play passes to a child from the other team when the child chooses to stop or when a 1 is rolled. If two 1s are rolled, the team's whole score goes back to zero. As the game progresses, discuss the probability of rolling a 1 or two 1s.

Mean, median and mode

Roll seven times

Split the class into two teams. Ask a child from Team A to roll a dice seven times. Write the results on the board. Ask the children to find the mode (or modal values), the median and the range. Write them on the board. Then ask a child from Team B to roll seven times, and again find the mode, median and range. Award a point for each of mode, median and range to the team that has the higher number. If appropriate, children can also be shown how to find the mean, using a calculator if necessary.

Scales of graphs and charts

Intervals

Draw a simple number scale on the board, for example, one showing the numbers 125, 150, 175 and 200. Ask a child to come to the board and draw a cross on the line to show a specified number, for example 154 or 167. Discuss strategies for being as accurate as possible, such as dividing each interval into parts. Remind the children that it is important to look at two adjacent numbers on the scale and find the difference, in order to find out what each interval is worth (in this case 25).

Databases

Initial birthday

Ask each child to state the first letter of their name and the month of their birthday, for example *F* and *Jan*. Compile a table on the board and ask questions such as: *How many children have their birthday in May? What is the most common initial letter? Are people with the letter L more likely to have a winter birthday than those with the letter B?* Discuss ways of organising the data so that it can be accessed easily, for example, sorting the information by name alphabetically or according to birthday months.

Easily accessible sources and further ideas

The following suggestions for real-life data can be used as a stimulus for further data work.

Newspapers These contain a wealth of information, for example: TV programme listings, football tables, sports results, temperature readings and weather reports. They can also be analysed with questions such as *How many letter As are in this report?*

Travel brochures Children can investigate temperatures, compare prices, find out which destinations have most hotels with swimming pools, and so on.

Magazines Look out for survey results presented in charts or graphs for the children to interpret, as well as questionnaires that the children can answer themselves.

The school and children themselves Investigate measurements of objects in school, different ball diameters, growth of houseplants/seedlings, children's standing jump results, cooking and food technology activities, activities children undertake at home or during holidays, and so on.

Calendars Children can analyse the information on calendars. Ask questions such as: *What day is the first/last/sixth of each month? In which month do most children in the class have a birthday?*

Useful websites
www.standards.dfes.gov.uk/numeracy
www.dinosaurworld.com/facts.html
www.metoffice.gov.uk/education/data
www.schoolhistory.co.uk
www.georesources.co.uk

The chances are...

- **Read each newspaper cutting carefully.**
- **Underline the** | probability | **words.**

Talk about them with a partner.

Mrs Wilson agreed to have the operation. She was told there was a <u>small risk</u>.

In all likelihood the match will be postponed tomorrow.

There is a 50-50 chance her baby will be a boy.

The manager said there was some doubt as to whether Beckham would play on Saturday.

There is little risk of catching the disease tuberculosis nowadays.

It is possible that the Spice Girls will sing together this evening at the gala concert.

Spurs have a good chance of winning as they are at home with no players injured.

It is probable that Saheel will pass her test.

Forecasters are still uncertain as to whether it will be a white Christmas.

Rain is very likely tomorrow.

- **Write some statements of your own using probability words.**

_____

_____

_____

_____

_____

Now try this!

Noughts and crosses is not a fair game as the person who goes first has a better chance of winning.

- **What does** | fair | **mean?**
- **Make two spinners, one that is fair and one that is unfair.**

Teachers' note Ensure the children realise that probability is related to whether or not something is impossible, certain or somewhere in between. The children's own statements can be grouped into things that are quite likely to happen and things that are unlikely to happen. They could even try to arrange the situations in order of chance. Discuss the meaning of 'fair' as 'equally likely to happen'.

Developing Numeracy Handling Data Year 5 © A & C Black 2002

6

Take a chance

• **Play this game with a partner.**

You each need a copy of this sheet.

You also need the cards from Chance cards: 1 and 2.

☆ Take turns to pick a card and read it.

☆ Decide on the **likelihood** of the statement. Cross this hump off your monster for Round 1.

☆ The first player to cross off all five humps in a round wins.

☆ If you disagree about one of the cards, put it to one side and pick a new card.

Round 1

no chance   poor chance   even chance   good chance   certain

Round 2

no chance   poor chance   even chance   good chance   certain

Round 3

impossible   unlikely   equally likely   likely   certain

Round 4

impossible   unlikely   equally likely   likely   certain

Now try this!

• **Write a statement of your own for each of these.**

good chance   unlikely   probable   likely   even chance   impossible

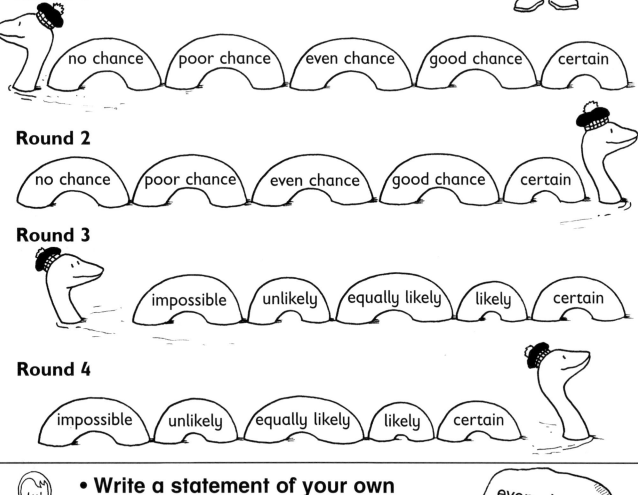

Teachers' note Use this with pages 8 and 9. As a further extension, ask children to choose or write a card for each 'hump' and to glue them along a probability line marked with words (you could enlarge the lines on page 43). Discuss that we cannot be entirely certain that something will happen, but that the chances can be almost certain. During the plenary, discuss contentious cards with the whole class.

Developing Numeracy Handling Data Year 5 © A & C Black 2002

• **Cut out the cards. Use them with the game Take a chance.**

You will turn into a frog this week. 	You will meet Prince William this year.
 One day you will learn to drive a car.	You will go to school this month.
If you roll a 1 to 6 dice you will get the number 10.	 Someone in your family will win the lottery.
A newborn baby will be a boy. 	Next year will be 1999. 
One day you will be a famous footballer.	If you toss a coin it will come down heads.
It will get light tomorrow.	It will rain before Sunday.
 Your teacher will tell you off this year.	If you roll a 1 to 6 dice you will get the number 6 first time.
Next Christmas Day will be on 25 December. 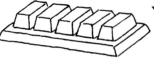	The day after Monday will be Friday.
Tomorrow you will go to the moon.	 You will eat some chocolate today.
You will get an ace when you pick from a pack of cards.	You will get a diamond when you pick from a pack of cards.
It will rain tomorrow. 	 It will get dark tonight.

Teachers' note Use this with pages 7 and 9. Before beginning, discuss the suits and numbers in a pack of playing cards. Ensure the children realise that the chances for some statements will vary for different people or places, for example, 'you will be a famous footballer' might be more likely for one person than for another and 'raining before Sunday' might be more likely in Britain than in a desert.

**Developing Numeracy
Handling Data Year 5
© A & C Black 2002**

Chance cards: 2

- **Cut out the cards. Use them with the game Take a chance.**

A person in your family will be eaten by a wolf today.

You will see the Loch Ness monster this year.

 On Sunday you will have some ice cream.

You will climb Mount Everest tomorrow.

If you roll a 1 to 6 dice you will get an odd number.

If you add an odd number to an even number, the answer will be odd.

A newborn baby will be a girl.

If you toss a coin it will come down tails.

 If you roll a 1 to 6 dice you will get an even number.

A day of this week will begin with the letter T.

You will see an owl this week.

On your way home you will see a car.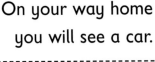

 Your teacher will drink something today.

Someone will be away from your class tomorrow.

 If you roll a 1 to 6 dice you will get a multiple of 3.

You will get a black card when you pick from a pack of cards.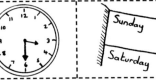

You'll leave school today between 15:00 and 16:00.

The day after Sunday will be Saturday.

You will get a red card when you pick from a pack of cards.

If you roll a 1 to 6 dice you will get a multiple of 2.

It will snow tomorrow.

It will rain sometime during this year.

Teachers' note Use this with pages 7 and 8. Before beginning, discuss the suits and numbers in a pack of playing cards. Ensure the children realise that the chances for some statements will vary for different people or places.

**Developing Numeracy
Handling Data Year 5
© A & C Black 2002**

9

Dicey decisions

• **Play this game with a partner.**

> **You need** a copy of this sheet each, and a 1 to 6 dice between you.

☆ Player 1: Roll the dice again and again, adding the numbers as you go. Stop whenever you like because if you roll a 6, you lose your whole score for this turn.

☆ If you stop before you roll a 6, add your score to your total. Then it is your partner's turn.

☆ If you roll a 6, write 'no score'. It is your partner's turn.

☆ The player with the most points after 8 turns wins.

• **Keep score like this:**

Dice rolls		Total
3 + 5 + 1	Stop = 9	9
2 + 6	No score	9

Dice rolls	Total	Dice rolls	Total

• **Discuss the strategies you used.**

> About how many times did you roll the dice on each turn?

> Did the numbers you had already rolled help you decide when to stop?

> Did you decide to stop once you reached a particular score? If so, what was that score?

• **Would it make any difference if the number 6 were changed to 5?**

Teachers' note Encourage the children to question their strategies and explain their reasoning. Some may begin to realise that the greater their current score, the more they have to lose by continuing. Children often incorrectly believe that if a 6 has not been rolled for a while it is more likely to come up than before (this is not true; the probability is always one sixth no matter what has been rolled before).

**Developing Numeracy
Handling Data Year 5**
© A & C Black 2002

Sweet surprise!

- Colour the sweets in the bags. Use at least three different colours in each bag.
- For each colour, work out the likelihood of picking that colour sweet from the bag. Mark a cross on the probability line.

You need
red, yellow, blue and green coloured pencils.

Use the coloured pencils to mark the crosses.

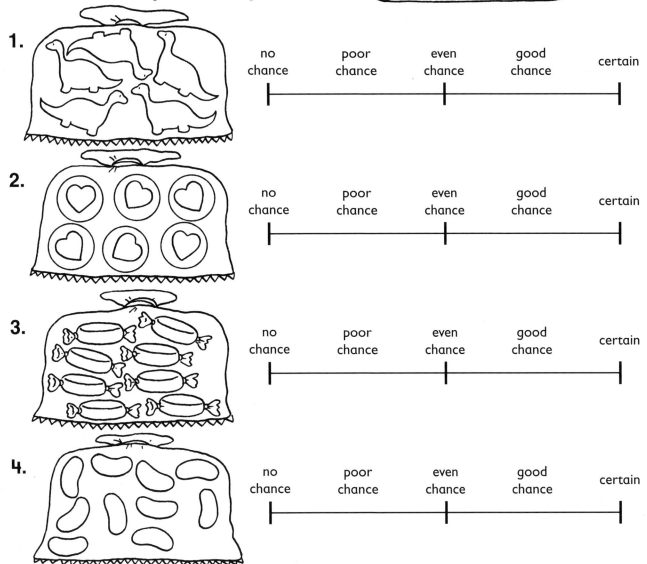

1.

no chance	poor chance	even chance	good chance	certain

2.

no chance	poor chance	even chance	good chance	certain

3.

no chance	poor chance	even chance	good chance	certain

4.

no chance	poor chance	even chance	good chance	certain

Now try this!

- **Draw your own bag with 12 sweets, where the chances are:**

no chance	even chance	certain

green red   blue yellow

Teachers' note Use a bag and coloured cubes to demonstrate what the activity is about. Using the blank scales on page 43, explain that the closer something is to the left-hand edge of the scale, the less likely it is, and vice versa for the right-hand edge. To help the children place their crosses accurately, ask them to imagine the line split into the number of equal parts that there are objects.

**Developing Numeracy
Handling Data Year 5
© A & C Black 2002**

Who's got flu?

A doctor wanted to know how many patients had flu in one year. She surveyed 100 people in each age group:

Age (years)	Months											
	J	F	M	A	M	J	J	A	S	O	N	D
0–10	11	13	9	5	2	1	0	0	0	5	9	15
11–20	8	7	5	3	1	0	0	0	0	4	6	9
21–30	6	6	4	3	2	1	0	0	1	3	5	8
31–40	7	6	3	3	3	2	0	0	0	2	5	6
41–50	9	8	9	5	4	2	0	0	0	3	6	9
51–60	10	8	11	8	5	3	0	0	1	5	3	7
Over 60	14	19	12	9	7	1	0	1	1	8	16	17

- **Look at the data. Read the sentences and fill in the missing words. Use** more likely, about as likely **and** less likely.

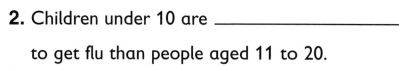

1. People are less likely to get flu in summer than in winter.
2. Children under 10 are ______________ to get flu than people aged 11 to 20.
3. People are ______________ to get flu in July than in December.
4. People are ______________ to get flu in August as in July.
5. People over 60 are ______________ to get flu than any other age group.
6. People are ______________ to get flu in April as in October.
7. People aged 21 to 30 are ______________ to get flu as people aged 31 to 40.

- **Write five more statements using this data.**

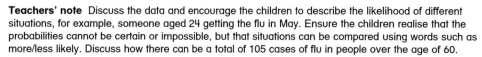

Teachers' note Discuss the data and encourage the children to describe the likelihood of different situations, for example, someone aged 24 getting the flu in May. Ensure the children realise that the probabilities cannot be certain or impossible, but that situations can be compared using words such as more/less likely. Discuss how there can be a total of 105 cases of flu in people over the age of 60.

Lucky talk

- **Talk to a partner about each statement. Say whether you agree with it or not.**

a Because it was wet today, it is likely to be dry tomorrow.

b Because the coin landed on heads this time, it is likely to land on tails next time.

c I picked the number 5 from a set of 1 to 6 number cards. I put it back in the pack and shuffled. I am less likely to pick the number 5 this time.

d Mrs Hill has a baby girl. Her next child is more likely to be a boy.

e Because the dice landed on a 6 this time, it is less likely to land on a 6 next time.

f Because my sister won the first game of cards we played, I am more likely to win the second game.

g I tossed a coin four times. Each time it landed heads side up. Next time it is much more likely to land tails side up.

h The lottery numbers this week are 6, 7, 15, 19, 35 and 39. This means these numbers are less likely to come up next week.

- **Write whether you agree or disagree with each statement. Explain your reasoning.**

a _____ _____

b _____ _____

c _____ _____

d _____ _____

e _____ _____

f _____ _____

g _____ _____

h _____ _____

Teachers' note The statements are all untrue, as the probability of such events happening is not altered by what happens previously, for example, the probability of rolling a 6 on a fair dice is always one sixth regardless of what was rolled previously. This is a difficult idea to grasp but can provoke some interesting reasoning. As an extension, the children could write their own statements to test.

**Developing Numeracy
Handling Data Year 5
© A & C Black 2002**

Dinosaur names

Ella and Tom are arguing about the length of dinosaur names.

Most dinosaurs have more than 10 letters in their name.

No! Most dinosaurs have 10 letters or fewer in their name.

- **Who do you think is right?** Ella ☐   Tom ☐   Can't tell ☐
- **Count the letters in the names. Draw a tally chart.**

Triceratops	Microceratops
Velociraptor	Diplodocus
Tyrannosaurus	Micropachycephalosaurus
Brachiosaurus	Charcharodontosaurus
Apatosaurus	Supersaurus
Utah Raptor	Echninoden
Seismosaurus	Archaeornithomimus
Oviraptor	Xiaosaurus
Argentinasaurus	Spinosaurus
Ultrasaurus	Minmi
Saltopus	Megalosaurus

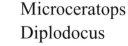

1. How many dinosaur names are in this list? _____

2. How many have more than 10 letters? _____

3. How many have 10 letters or fewer? _____

Here is some more useful information.

About 750 kinds of dinosaur have been named.
The longest name is Micropachycephalosaurus. It has 23 letters.
The shortest name is Minmi. It has 5 letters.

- **Do you think Ella or Tom is right, or do you still need more information?** _____

- **Give your reasons.** _____

_____

Teachers' note Encourage the children to discuss Ella and Tom's statements, including what information would be required to prove one of them without doubt. As an extension activity, you could introduce grouped data. Ask the children to draw a bar chart showing the information, where the horizontal axis shows the number of letters grouped into 1–5, 6–10, 11–15, 16–20 and 21–25 letters.

**Developing Numeracy
Handling Data Year 5
© A & C Black 2002**

Frequency and mode

Frequency means how many times something occurs.

• **Look at this advert.**

'Lighter white' toothpaste
'Lighter white' toothpaste makes teeth clean and white!
'Lighter white' makes brighter white teeth.

There are eight different words in this advert.

• **List them below. Write the frequency of each word.**

lighter	3						

• **Which word is the** mode **in this advert?**

The most common thing or number in a set is called the **mode**.

_____

• **Write your own advert where the word** fresh **is the mode. Do not use more than nine different words.**

Your advert can be for anything!

• **List the different words in your advert. Write the frequency of each word.**

Now try this!

• **Draw a bar chart to show the data for your advert.**

Frequency

Words

Teachers' note Encourage the children to make their own adverts as long as possible. They should use the nine words as many times as they can, while ensuring the word 'fresh' is the mode. For the extension, the children could use the blank bar chart on page 45. As a further extension, ask them to write five statements about the data in their charts. They can also look up the frequency of words in real adverts.

Developing Numeracy
Handling Data Year 5
© **A & C Black 2002**

15

Soap survey

• **How many soaps do you watch regularly?** ☐

Neighbours, EastEnders, Coronation Street...

• **Find out how many soaps the children in your class watch.**

• **Fill in this tally chart.**

Number of soaps watched	Tally	Frequency (total)
0		
1		
2		
3		
4		
5		
6		

1. How many children took part in the survey? _____

• **Draw a bar chart.**

• **Use it to answer the questions.**

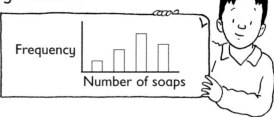

Frequency

Number of soaps

2. How many children watch: **(a)** 3 soaps? _____ **(b)** no soaps? _____

   (c) more than 4 soaps? _____   **(d)** fewer than 3 soaps? _____

3. How many more children watch 2 soaps than 5 soaps? _____

4. If an episode of each soap lasts half an hour, and there are five episodes a

   week, for how many hours a week would you watch:

   (a) 1 soap? _____ hrs   **(b)** 2 soaps? _____ hrs   **(c)** 3 soaps? _____ hrs

   (d) 4 soaps? _____ hrs   **(e)** 5 soaps? _____ hrs   **(f)** 6 soaps? _____ hrs

Now try this!

• **Find the mode for the number of soaps watched.** _____

Teachers' note After allowing thinking time, call out the children's names in turn and ask them to say the number of soaps they watch. As numbers are called out, all children should mark the 'vote' as a tally in the appropriate section of the table. Mark your own copy for reference. Ensure the children realise that 'frequency' here means the number of people watching. A blank bar chart is available on page 45.

**Developing Numeracy
Handling Data Year 5
© A & C Black 2002**

Braille letters

Each letter of the Braille alphabet is made up of raised dots.

a	b	c	d	e	f	g	h	i	j	k	l	m

n	o	p	q	r	s	t	u	v	w	x	y	z

- Fill in the tally chart to show how many letters are made from each number of dots.

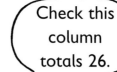
Check this column totals 26.

Number of dots	Tally	Frequency
1		
2		
3		
4		
5		
6		

1. How many Braille letters are made from:

(a) 3 dots? _____   (b) 5 dots? _____

(c) 6 dots? _____   (d) 1 dot? _____   (e) 2 dots? _____

(f) more than 3 dots? _____   (g) more than 2 dots? _____

(h) fewer than 3 dots? _____   (i) fewer than 4 dots? _____

2. How many more letters are made from 3 dots than 5 dots? _____

3. Why do you think only one letter is made from 1 dot?

_____

4. Which are the two most common numbers of dots per letter

(the modes)? _____

Now try this!

- **Invent your own alphabet using crosses. Use from 3 to 9 crosses for each letter and make them all different. Make the mode for the number of crosses equal 6.**

Teachers' note Discuss the purpose and use of the Braille alphabet and, if possible, let the children feel some pages of it. Revise the term 'mode' and ensure the children realise that there can be more than one mode or modal value. As a further extension, the children could draw bar charts for their own alphabet, using the blank bar chart on page 45.

Developing Numeracy
Handling Data Year 5
© A & C Black 2002

17

Ice skates

If your class went to the ice rink, how many pairs of ice skates in each size would you need? Let's find out!

- **Write your name on a piece of paper. Place it at the front of the class next to your shoe size.**
- **Use the data about shoe sizes to fill in this table.**

Shoe sizes								
Number of children								

- **Draw a bar chart like this:**

Frequency

Shoe sizes

1. What is the total number of children in your survey? _____

2. **(a)** Which is the most common shoe size? _____

   (b) Do you think the ice rink should have more skates in this size than any other? Why? _____

   _____

3. Which is the least common shoe size? _____

4. If three Year 5 classes go skating at the same time, about how many pairs of skates will they need in:

   (a) size 13? _____   **(b)** size 2? _____

Now try this!

- **Imagine <u>you</u> own the ice rink. You can hire out 200 pairs of skates.**
- **How many pairs of skates in each size would you have? Write a list.**

Explain your list to the rest of the class.

Teachers' note Place labels at the front of the class showing shoe sizes, for the children to place their name cards alongside. The name cards can then be counted and recorded. Allow time for children who have completed the extension activity to explain their lists. Discuss possible scenarios of ages of people skating and, if possible, gather more data about shoe sizes of other children and adults.

Developing Numeracy Handling Data Year 5 © A & C Black 2002

Speed typing

In a 'sponsored type', each child had to type the alphabet as many times as they could in five minutes.

Some children in Year 5 had a trial run two weeks before. This bar chart shows their results.

The children practised over the two weeks. This bar chart shows their results on the 'sponsored type' day.

Notice that the scale of this chart is different from the one above.

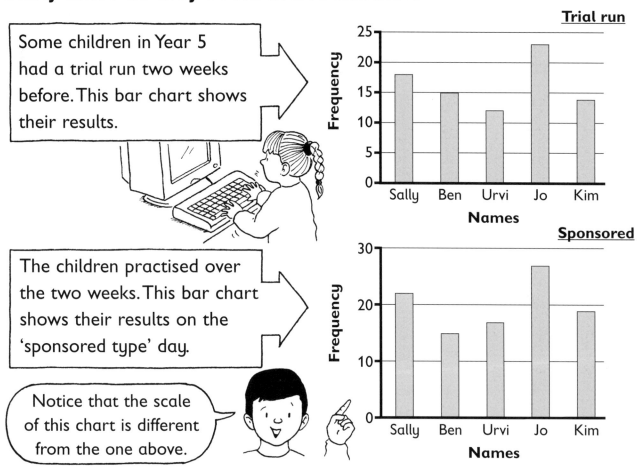

• **Compare the two charts. Fill in the table.**

Child's name	Trial run score	Sponsored score	Improvement? By how many?

Now try this!

• **Write a report of the results. You could start like this:**

Five children from Year 5 did a typing test and then repeated it two weeks later. Sally scored _____ in her first test. With practice she improved. She scored _____ in her second test, which was an improvement of _____ ...

Teachers' note Encourage discussion about which of the five children made the greatest and smallest improvement. Children in the class could try this typing activity themselves and show the results of a group in a similar way. If computers are not available, the children could see how many times they can write the alphabet in five minutes.

**Developing Numeracy
Handling Data Year 5**
© A & C Black 2002

Hair Flair

- **Look at the** bar line chart **. It shows the number of clients in the Hair Flair salon on each hour between 8 am and 5 pm.**

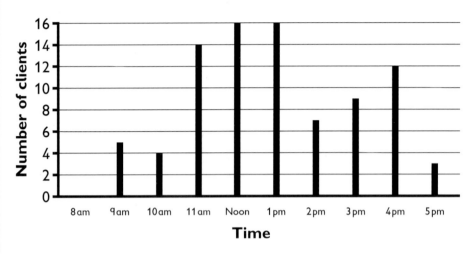

1. How many clients were in the salon at:

   (a) 9 am? __5__ **(b)** noon? _____ **(c)** 2 pm? _____ **(d)** 4 pm? _____

2. Between which two hours do you think the hairdressers were most busy? _____

3. How many more clients were there at 11 am than at 2 pm? _____

4. How many fewer clients were there at 9 am than at 4 pm? _____

5. Do you think there were ever more than 16 clients in the salon at the same time during this day? Why?_____

_____

6. What time do you think the salon might have opened? Why? _____

_____

7. How many hairdressers do you think needed to work on this day, if one hairdresser worked with each client? _____

- **If there are 20 hairdressers, work out the best times for each of them to have a lunch hour.**

Teachers' note This sheet requires the children to use their initiative when answering some of the questions. As only the numbers of clients *on* the hour are given, definite assumptions cannot be made about the numbers in between. Encourage the children to discuss the chart with a partner. Ask simple questions such as *How many more/fewer clients were there at ... than at ...?*

**Developing Numeracy
Handling Data Year 5**
© A & C Black 2002

Dino data

The bar line chart shows the lengths of six different dinosaurs.

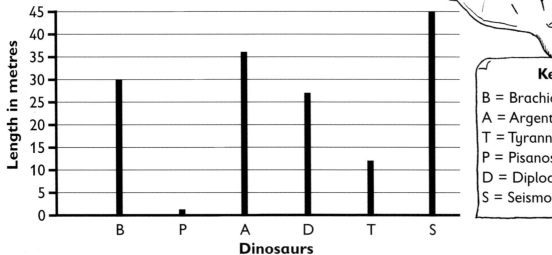

Key

B = Brachiosaurus
A = Argentinasaurus
T = Tyrannosaurus
P = Pisanosaurus
D = Diplodocus
S = Seismosaurus

1. Write the approximate length of:

Brachiosaurus ___30___ m   Pisanosaurus _____ m

Argentinasaurus _____ m   Diplodocus _____ m

Tyrannosaurus _____ m   Seismosaurus _____ m

• **Measure the length of your classroom.**

Length = _____ m

You need a metre stick.

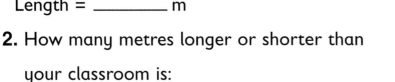

2. How many metres longer or shorter than

your classroom is:

Brachiosaurus? _____ m   Pisanosaurus? _____ m

Argentinasaurus? _____ m   Diplodocus? _____ m

3. What is the **range** of

dinosaur lengths? _____ m

The **range** is the difference between the shortest and the longest length.

Now try this!

• **Work in a group of six. Measure how far each of you can stretch your body along the floor. Draw a bar line chart of the information.**

Teachers' note Tell the children that the Seismosaurus is the longest dinosaur known, and the Micropachycephalosaurus is the shortest at 50 cm long. Encourage them to compare these lengths with real-life objects and spaces. For the extension activity, the children can use the blank bar line chart on page 46. Suggest that they label the vertical axis 'Length' and the horizontal axis 'Name'.

**Developing Numeracy
Handling Data Year 5
© A & C Black 2002**

Fat free?

The bar line chart shows the number of grams of fat in every 100 grams of different foods.

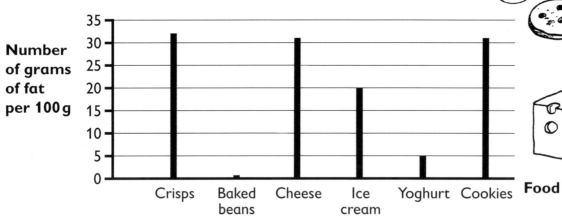

Number of grams of fat per 100 g

1. How many more grams of fat are there in 100 g of:

(a) cookies than yoghurt? _____ g   (b) crisps than beans? _____ g

2. In 100 g, which food has:

(a) the least fat? _____   (b) the most fat? _____

3. A bag of crisps contains 25 g of crisps.

(a) If you eat 100 g of crisps, how many bags is this? _____

(b) How many grams of fat are in one bag of crisps? _____ g

The recommended amount of fat to eat each day is 70 g for a woman and 95 g for a man.

4. If a woman and a man ate only crisps for a day, how many whole bags could they eat without going over the recommended amount?

(a) woman _____   (b) man _____

Now try this!

• **Read the number of grams of fat per 100 g for these spreads. Draw a bar line chart to show the data.**

| Better Butter 81 g | Sunflower 38 g | Utter Butter 67 g |
| Golden 60 g | Slimlight 23 g | Vitality 63 g | Superspread 38 g |

Teachers' note Discuss that it is not a good idea to eat just one food type in a day! Ask further questions, for example: *A 400 g tin of baked beans contains how much fat? How many tins could a man eat in a day without going over the recommended amount?* Look at food packets and compare other nutritional data such as protein or carbohydrates. A blank bar line chart is available on page 46.

**Developing Numeracy
Handling Data Year 5
© A & C Black 2002**

Drinks machine

The bar line chart shows the number of cans in a drinks machine.

The machine holds 100 cans when full.

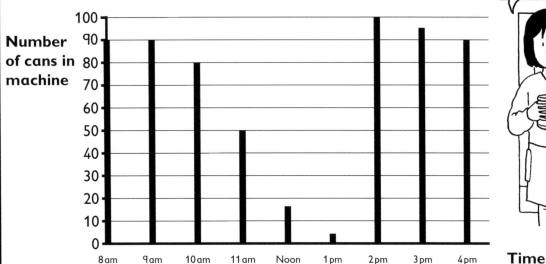

Number of cans in machine

Time

1. How many cans were sold between: **(a)** 8 am and 9 am? ___0___

   (b) 9 am and 10 am? _____   **(c)** 10 am and 11 am? _____

   (d) 11 am and noon? _____   **(e)** noon and 1 pm? _____

   (f) 2 pm and 3 pm? _____   **(g)** 3 pm and 4 pm? _____

2. Between which two hours were the most cans sold? _____

3. Why do you think no cans were sold between 8 am and 9 am?

   _____

4. What do you think happened between 1 pm and 2 pm?

   _____

5. Where might this drinks machine be? _____

6. Do you think many cans are sold between 4 pm and 8 am? Why?

   _____

   _____

Now try this!

• **Now draw a bar line chart to show**

   a day in the life of a chocolate bar machine .

Teachers' note Encourage the children to discuss the graph with a partner. Ask simple questions such as: *How many cans were in the machine at ten/eleven/twelve o'clock? How many more/fewer cans were in the machine at ... than at ...?* The children could write a story about a day in the life of this drinks machine. For the extension activity, the children can use the blank bar line chart on page 46.

Developing Numeracy
Handling Data Year 5
© A & C Black 2002

Travelling light

Mr Glow is a salesman. He sells solar panels around the country. This is the story of his week.

> On Monday I went from Bristol to Dover, on Tuesday from Dover to Manchester and on Wednesday from Manchester to Glasgow. On Thursday I stayed in Glasgow. On Friday I travelled from Glasgow to Aberdeen, on Saturday from Aberdeen to Manchester, and then on Sunday from Manchester back to Bristol.

• **The chart shows the number of miles between cities. Use it to help you answer the questions.**

	Aberdeen	Bristol	Dover	Glasgow	Manchester
Aberdeen	——	490	574	150	332
Bristol	490	——	195	366	167
Dover	574	195	——	467	265
Glasgow	150	366	467	——	210
Manchester	332	167	265	210	——

1. How many miles did Mr Glow travel on: **(a)** Monday? __195__

   (b) Tuesday? _____ **(c)** Wednesday? _____ **(d)** Thursday? _____

   (e) Friday? _____ **(f)** Saturday? _____ **(g)** Sunday? _____

2. (a) What was the furthest he travelled in one day? _____ miles

   (b) On which day was this? _____

3. On which day did he not travel? _____

4. How many more miles did he travel:

   (a) on Wednesday than on Monday? _____

   (b) on Tuesday than on Sunday? _____

5. Use a calculator to work out how far he travelled during the week. _____ miles

• **Draw a bar line chart of Mr Glow's travels.**

Teachers' note Ensure that the children understand how to read the chart. For the extension activity, a blank bar line chart is available on page 46. Encourage the children to use a vertical scale marked in 100s (with one division representing 25 miles). Some children could also draw a bar line chart to show how far from Bristol Mr Glow was each night, for example, on Monday he was in Dover so he was 195 miles away.

**Developing Numeracy
Handling Data Year 5
© A & C Black 2002**

Whitby Town

The bar line chart shows the league position of Whitby Town football club during the last ten weeks of the season.

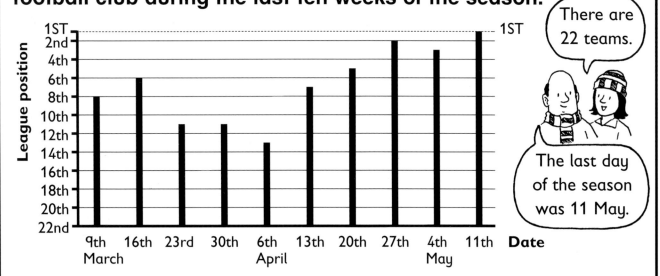

There are 22 teams.

The last day of the season was 11 May.

1. In which position were Whitby on: **(a)** 9 March? ___8th___

(b) 20 April? _____   **(c)** the last day of the season? _____

2. On which date were Whitby in: **(a)** 6th position? _____

(b) 3rd position? _____   **(c)** their lowest position? _____

3. By how many positions did the team **rise** between

6 April and 13 April? _____

4. By how many positions did the team **fall** between

16 March and 23 March? _____

5. For how many weeks were they below 6th position? _____

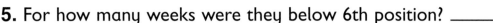

Now try this!

The table shows the league position of Scarborough.

Date	9 Mar	16 Mar	23 Mar	30 Mar	6 Apr	13 Apr	20 Apr	27 Apr	4 May	11 May
Position	14th	15th	17th	13th	11th	12th	16th	19th	21st	22nd

- **Draw a bar line chart to show this information.**
- **Compare the bar line charts. When were Scarborough in a higher position than Whitby?** _____

Teachers' note Discuss with the children that the vertical scale on this bar line chart shows league positions from 22nd up to 1st. Compare this chart with other bar line charts and emphasise the importance of looking closely at the scales. Children could visit their favourite club's website to find data and draw a bar line chart of 10 weeks in a season. A blank bar line chart is available on page 46.

**Developing Numeracy
Handling Data Year 5
© A & C Black 2002**

Elephants

The bar line charts show the growth rates of male and female African elephants.

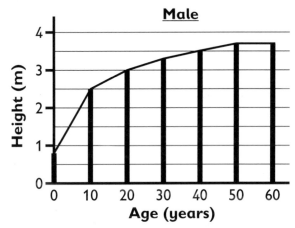

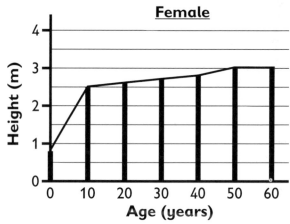

1. About how tall is a male elephant aged:

   (a) 10? _2·5_ m   **(b)** 20? _____ m   **(c)** 30? _____ m   **(d)** 50? _____ m

2. About how tall is a female elephant aged:

   (a) 10? _____ m   **(b)** 20? _____ m   **(c)** 30? _____ m   **(d)** 50? _____ m

3. At what age do the elephants stop growing? _____

4. Between which ages is a female elephant the same size as a male elephant?

   between _____ and _____ years

• **Compare the two charts. Write as many similarities and differences as you can between the growth rates of male and female elephants.**

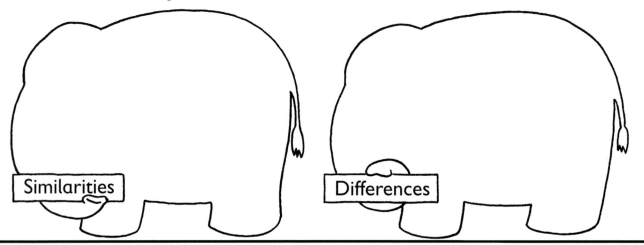

Similarities

Differences

Teachers' note Discuss why the bar lines on these graphs are joined. Encourage the children to find out more about African and Indian elephants from books or the Internet. Indian elephants are smaller in size, growing to a maximum height of between 2 and 3·5 m. Children could produce similar charts (using the blank bar line chart on page 46) for Indian elephants, or other animals, and compare them.

**Developing Numeracy
Handling Data Year 5
© A & C Black 2002**

Don't be fooled!

These four bar line charts show the amount of money in Ravi's pocket at noon each day, over a four-week period.

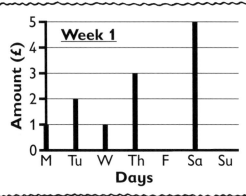
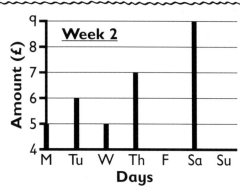
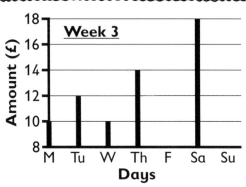
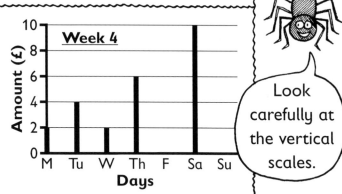

Look carefully at the vertical scales.

• **Read the statements. Write** ⬚true⬚**,** ⬚false⬚ **or** ⬚don't know⬚ **for each week.**

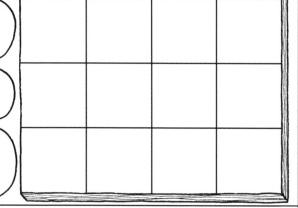

	Week 1	Week 2	Week 3	Week 4
1. I had no money on Friday.	true			
2. I had twice as much money on Tuesday as on Wednesday.				
3. I had £1 less on Wednesday than on Tuesday.				
4. I had more money on Wednesday and Thursday put together than I had on Saturday.				

Now try this!

• **What do the vertical scales on the charts for weeks 1 and 4 have in common?** _____

Teachers' note Before the children begin, ask them to describe the similarities and differences between the bar line charts. Stress the importance of not being 'fooled' by the charts and of examining the scales carefully. The children should write 'don't know' only if it is not possible to tell. Encourage them to draw their own charts which look similar but have different scales, and to write statements.

**Developing Numeracy
Handling Data Year 5
© A & C Black 2002**

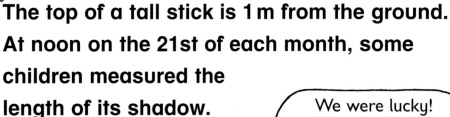

Shadow stick

The top of a tall stick is 1 m from the ground.
At noon on the 21st of each month, some
children measured the
length of its shadow.

We were lucky!
Every time we did this,
the sun was shining.

Here are the results, in centimetres.

J	F	M	A	M	J	J	A	S	O	N	D
370	260	150	100	80	60	80	100	150	260	370	430

- **Draw a bar line chart of the information.**
- **Join the tops of the bar lines.**

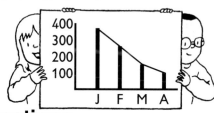

- **Use your bar line chart to answer the questions.**

1. In which month was the shadow:

  (a) the longest? <u>December</u>   **(b)** the shortest? _____

2. Was the shadow longer in August or in May? _____

- **Draw a line across your graph
  to show 100 cm (1 metre).**

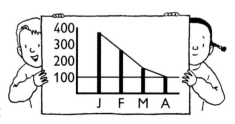

3. For how many months was the shadow:

  (a) less than 1 m? _____   **(b)** more than 1 m? _____

4. The shadow was 2 m at two times of the year. When?

      between _____ and _____

  and between _____ and _____

Now try this!

- **How long do you think the shadow would be if
  <u>you</u> did the experiment this week?** _____ cm

Teachers' note Discuss the path of the sun at different times of the year and the reason for this (the earth is tilted and the sun's rays fall on the northern hemisphere more directly in summer than in winter). Discuss why the bar lines are joined in the example graphs. A blank bar line chart is available on page 46. The children may need help with labelling the vertical scale.

**Developing Numeracy
Handling Data Year 5
© A & C Black 2002**

Shadow stick

The top of a tall stick is 1 m from the ground.
At noon on the 21st of each month, some
children measured the
length of its shadow.

> We were lucky!
> Every time we did this,
> the sun was shining.

Here are the results, in centimetres.

J	F	M	A	M	J	J	A	S	O	N	D
370	260	150	100	80	60	80	100	150	260	370	430

• **Draw a bar line chart of the information.**

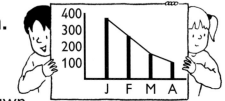

• **Join the tops of the bar lines.**

1. Describe the shape of the line you have just drawn.

_____

2. (a) In which month was the shadow the longest? _____

    (b) What does this tell you about the position of the sun during this

        month? _____

3. (a) In which month was the shadow the shortest? _____

    (b) What does this tell you about the position of the sun during this

        month? _____

4. For about how many months was the shadow:

    (a) shorter than 1·5 m? _____   **(b)** longer than 2 m? _____

Now try
this!

Josh lives in the southern hemisphere.

• **Draw his measurements on your**
  bar line chart in a different colour.

J	F	M	A	M	J	J	A	S	O	N	D
80	100	150	260	370	430	370	260	150	100	80	60

Teachers' note Discuss the path of the sun at different times of the year and the reason for this (the earth is tilted and the sun's rays fall on the northern hemisphere more directly in summer than in winter). Discuss that when it is summer in the southern hemisphere it is winter in the northern hemisphere, and vice versa. A blank bar line chart is available on page 46.

**Developing Numeracy
Handling Data Year 5
© A & C Black 2002**

You've been framed! 1

A suspect was followed from outside a police station at 8 am. The line graph shows the distance of the suspect from the police station over a 12-hour period.

The railway station is 4 km from the police station.

The bank is 14 km from the police station.

The police arrested the suspect at 5 pm and took him to the police station.

Right outside the police station is a park bench.

6 km from the police station is the suspect's mother's house.

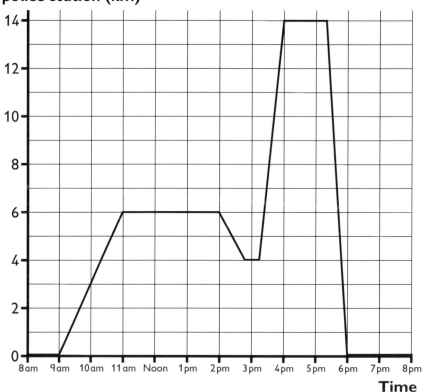

Distance from police station (km)

Time

- **Cut out the cards.**

- **Using the information above, arrange them in order.**

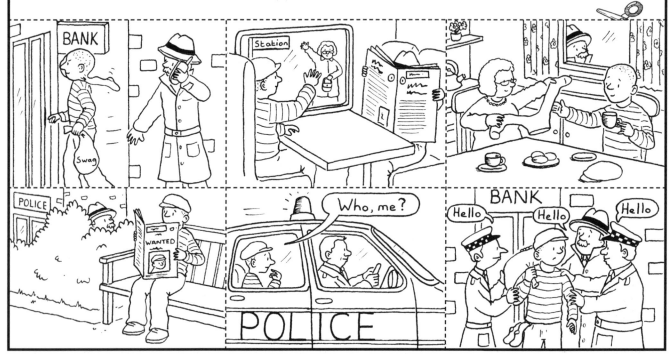

Teachers' note Before ordering the cards, the children could write the initials of each place on the vertical axis of the graph. The following sheet encourages the children to respond to more precise questions about this line graph.

**Developing Numeracy
Handling Data Year 5
© A & C Black 2002**

You've been framed! 2

You need the sheet called You've been framed! 1.

• Follow the trail. Answer the questions about the line graph.

1. At what time did the suspect reach his mum's house?

11:00 am

2. How long had it taken him to get there?

_____

3. How long did he spend at his mum's house?

_____

4. At about what time did he reach the railway station?

_____

6. Where was he at 4:00 pm?

_____

5. For about how long did he wait for a train?

_____

7. For how long did he sit on the bench outside the police station?

_____

8. About how long did his journey in the police car last?

_____

9. How far did he travel in the police car?

_____

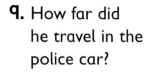

10. For how long was he away from the police station?

_____

• **Work out the total distance the suspect travelled between 8 am and 8 pm.** _____

Find the total of his four journeys.

Teachers' note To complete this sheet, the children will need a copy of page 30. As a further extension, ask the children to write or tell the story of the suspect's day, referring to the exact time of each event and its duration. They can include the pictures and graphs with their final presentations.

Developing Numeracy
Handling Data Year 5
© A & C Black 2002

When's summer?

The line graph shows the average temperature for each month in Edinburgh.

1. Which month is the warmest? _____

2. What is the temperature in May? _____

3. How much warmer is it in March than in December? _____

4. In which month is the temperature 12 °C? _____

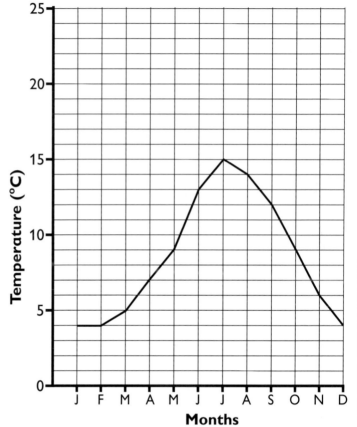

Temperature (°C)

Months

Here are the average temperatures in Perth, Australia.

J	F	M	A	M	J	J	A	S	O	N	D
23	23	22	19	16	14	13	13	15	16	19	22

• **Plot these points on the line graph. Join them with a line.**

Use a different colour.

5. During which months do you think it is summer in Perth?

_____ to _____

6. In which months is the temperature higher in Edinburgh than in Perth? _____

Now try this!

• **List as many differences as you can between the temperatures in Edinburgh and in Perth.**

Teachers' note Discuss what an average temperature is and ensure children realise that the daily temperatures throughout a month vary; some days are warmer/cooler than others. The average temperatures of other places could also be explored. The graph here could alternatively have been drawn as a bar line chart, but line graphs are commonly used in the media to show trends.

**Developing Numeracy
Handling Data Year 5
© A & C Black 2002**

Hot stuff

The line graph shows the temperature
of Mrs Smith's oven during a day.

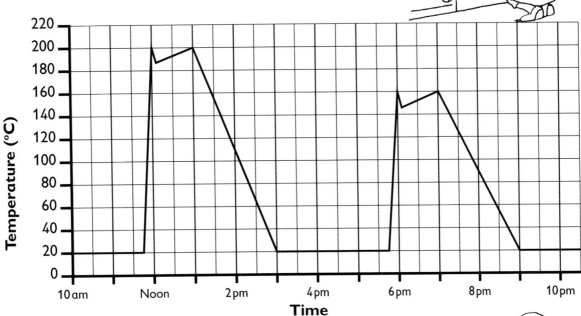

1. (a) What was the hottest temperature? _200 °C_

   (b) At what times was this? _____ and _____

2. At about what times did she:

   (a) turn the oven on? _____ and _____

   (b) turn the oven off? _____ and _____

3. For about how long was the oven switched on in total? _____

4. At approximately what times do you think Mrs Smith and her

   family ate? _____ and _____

5. Why do you think the temperature dropped slightly at noon and 6 pm?

   _____

6. On a separate sheet, write a story of what you think Mrs Smith

   might have been doing between 10 am and 10 pm.

Now try this!

- **For about how long was the oven temperature hotter
  than 100 °C?** _____

Teachers' note Ask the children why the temperature in the oven starts at 20 °C, not 0 °C (20 °C is
room temperature). Encourage them to discuss the story of Mrs Smith's day in pairs first, including
their own creative descriptions of other things she may have done! Children could consult recipes and
sketch their own oven line graphs with descriptions of different foods being cooked.

**Developing Numeracy
Handling Data Year 5
© A & C Black 2002**

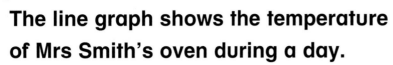

Hot stuff

The line graph shows the temperature of Mrs Smith's oven during a day.

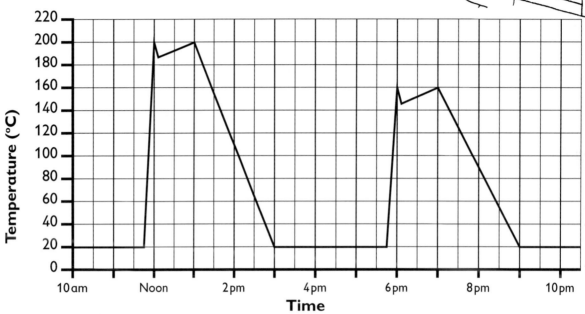

1. What was the temperature at:

    (a) 12 noon? _200 °C_   **(b)** 6 pm? _____

    (c) 2 pm? _____   **(d)** 10 pm? _____

2. Estimate the temperature at:

    (a) 8 pm _____   **(b)** 1 pm _____

    (c) 1:30 pm _____   **(d)** 7:30 pm _____

3. For approximately how long was the oven hotter than:

    (a) 160 °C? _____   **(b)** 120 °C? _____

4. Write the approximate times that the oven was at:

    (a) 180 °C _____

    (b) 60 °C _____

5. On a separate sheet, write a story of what you think Mrs Smith

    might have been doing between 10 am and 10 pm.

Now try this!

- **Estimate the times you think food was in the oven. Explain your reasoning.**

Teachers' note Ask the children why the temperature in the oven starts at 20 °C, not 0 °C (20 °C is room temperature). Encourage them to discuss the story of Mrs Smith's day in pairs first, including their own creative descriptions of other things she may have done! Children could consult recipes and sketch their own oven line graphs with descriptions of different foods being cooked.

**Developing Numeracy
Handling Data Year 5**
© A & C Black 2002

Hospital drama

The line graph shows Kim's temperature. It was recorded at 8 am and 8 pm each day.

The straight line shows the average normal temperature.

The vertical scale does not start at zero.

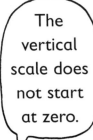

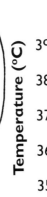

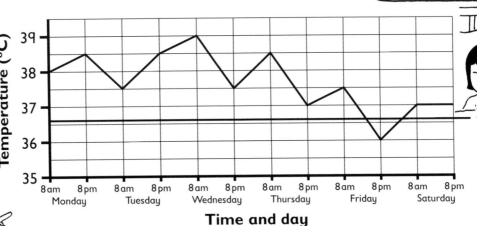

1. (a) What was Kim's **highest** recorded temperature? ___39 °C___

   (b) What day and time was this? _____

2. (a) What was Kim's **lowest** recorded temperature? _____

   (b) What day and time was this? _____

3. What was Kim's temperature at: (a) 8 am on Thursday? _____

   (b) 8 am on Friday? _____

   (c) 8 pm on Wednesday? _____

   (d) 8 pm on Tuesday? _____

4. By how many degrees did Kim's recorded temperature **rise** between:

   (a) Tuesday morning and Wednesday morning? _____

   (b) Wednesday evening and Thursday morning? _____

5. By how many degrees did Kim's recorded temperature **fall** between:

   (a) Monday evening and Tuesday morning? _____

   (b) Friday morning and Friday evening? _____

Now try this!

• **Estimate for how many hours Kim's temperature was below normal.** _____

Teachers' note Encourage the children to discuss in pairs the story of Kim's illness. Remind them to study the scales of any graph carefully, and ensure they do not make the mistake of thinking that Kim's temperature was double the normal temperature, just because the graph might 'look like that'. Discuss that Kim's temperature was taken only twice a day and might have been higher or lower at other times.

Developing Numeracy
Handling Data Year 5
© A & C Black 2002

School's out!

Six children finished school at 3:00 pm. The line graphs show how far from school each child went during the following hour.

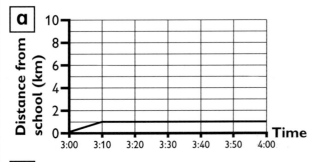

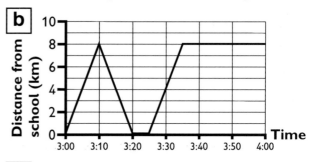

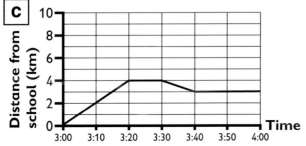

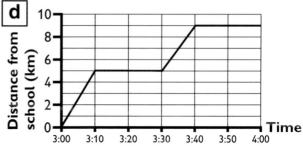

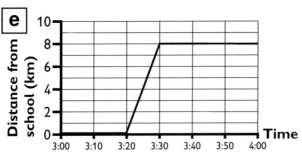

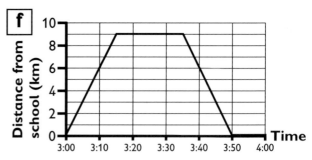

• **Match the graphs to the children. Write the letters in the boxes.**

1. I walked home and stayed in all evening.

2. I cycled home. After 10 minutes I walked back to my friend's house which I had passed on my way home.

3. Mum was 20 minutes late! She eventually arrived and drove me home.

4. Mum drove me home. I went back to school for Brownies at 4:00.

5. Dad drove me home, then drove me straight back to school – I'd forgotten my homework!

• **Write a story for the graph that is left.**

Teachers' note Ask the children more questions about the graphs, for example, the time each child arrived home and how far each child lives from school. Discuss that when the line on the graph is steep, it means that a lot of distance has been covered in a short time. As a further extension, the children could draw a graph showing their own travels during the hour after school on a particular day.

**Developing Numeracy
Handling Data Year 5
© A & C Black 2002**

36

Census records

Every ten years, a record is taken of all the people in the United Kingdom. This is called a census.

• Read this page from the census of 1861.

No. or name of house	Name and surname of each person	Relation to head of family	Condition as to marriage	Age Male	Age Female	Rank, profession or occupation	Where born
HIGHGATE FARM	ROBERT HARRISON	HEAD	MARRIED	49		FARMER	WHITBY
	HANNAH HARRISON	WIFE	MARRIED		45	HOUSEKEEPER	HAWSKER
	MARGARET HARRISON	DAU	U/M		17	DOM. SERVANT	HAWSKER
	HANNAH E. HARRISON	DAU	U/M		8	SCHOLAR	HAWSKER
	JOHN HARRISON	SON	U/M	4			HAWSKER
	J. THOMAS HARRISON	SON	U/M	2			HAWSKER
SALTGATE FARM	MATTHEW STEVENSON	HEAD	MARRIED	35		FARMER	HAWSKER
	MARY STEVENSON	WIFE	MARRIED		33	HOUSEKEEPER	SNEATON
	WILLIAM HERBERT	NEPHEW	U/M	24		LABOURER	HAWSKER

The data in this database can be sorted to find:

everyone under 10 years | people born in Hawsker | all the unmarried people | females between 10 and 20 years | all the wives | all the farmers

1. Using the database, find the number of:

   (a) wives _____   **(b)** farmers _____   **(c)** unmarried people _____

   (d) children under 10 _____   **(e)** people born in Hawsker _____

   (f) females between 10 and 20 years _____

2. Name: **(a)** the 45-year-old housekeeper _____

   (b) Matthew Stevenson's nephew _____

   (c) a person born in Sneaton _____

Now try this!

• **Make a database of characters from your favourite book.**

Teachers' note This page can be used to introduce databases, and to help children appreciate how useful it is to set out information in this way. Here the information includes both numerical and non-numerical data. Explain the abbreviations in the census and, if appropriate, discuss the issue of data protection. For the extension activity, the children could use the blank database on page 44.

**Developing Numeracy
Handling Data Year 5
© A & C Black 2002**

Hair today

Your teacher will give you a database sheet to help you test these statements:

Most girls in our class have hair that is between 10cm and 20cm long.

Most boys in our class have hair that is shorter than 6cm.

Parvati

Craig

☆ Work with a partner. Measure each other's hair length in centimetres. If the hair is different lengths, measure the longest part of the hair.

Don't forget that zero is sometimes part-way along a ruler!

My hair length is _____ cm.

☆ As each person says their hair length, write it in the second column of the database sheet.

☆ In the third column, write **M** or **F** to stand for 'male' or 'female'.

1. In your class, who has: **(a)** the longest hair? _____

(b) the shortest hair? _____

2. The **range** is the difference between the longest and the shortest hair lengths. Find the range of all the data. _____ cm

☆ Sort the information into a boy's list and a girl's list. Find out whether Parvati's and Craig's statements are true or false.

3. Explain your findings. _____

_____

_____

_____

4. Find the range of: **(a)** the girls' hair lengths. _____ cm

(b) the boys' hair lengths. _____ cm

Now try this!

• **Write two statements about the girls' hair lengths.**
• **Write two statements about the boys' hair lengths.**

Teachers' note Fill in the first column of the database on page 44 with the names of all the children in your class in alphabetical order. Give each child a photocopy. Once the children have measured their hair, call out the names and ask each child to say their hair length for all the children to record. Keep a record yourself. Some children could draw simple bar charts of the information using grouped data.

**Developing Numeracy
Handling Data Year 5
© A & C Black 2002**

Testing times

• **Try these tests.**

Your teacher will tell you when to start and when to stop.

Test 1 This sentence is written backwards. Write it forwards.

.eert egral a rednu gnittis tac a was yeht nehw

daor eht nwod gniklaw erew nerdlihc lareves yad enO

Start here

O _____

_____

_____

I wrote _____ words correctly.

Test 2 Add these digits.

302541 _15_   528195 _____   612941 _____   555555 _____

512215 _____   372018 _____   708590 _____   648694 _____

848555 _____   678495 _____   289489 _____   947895 _____

987968 _____   786967 _____   885769 _____   678895 _____

I added _____ sets of digits correctly.

Most of our class will score at least 9 in Test 1, and 7 in Test 2.

Your teacher will give you a database sheet to help you test this statement.

• **As your teacher calls out each name, fill in the results for Tests 1 and 2.**

Name	Test 1	Test 2
∿∿	∿	∿
∿∿		
∿∿		

• **Write the scores for** Test 1 **in order.**

Which score is the mode? _____

What is the range of scores? _____

• **Write the scores for** Test 2 **in order.**

Which score is the mode? _____

What is the range of scores? _____

Teachers' note Fill in the first column of the database on page 44 with the names of all the children in your class. Give each child a photocopy. Ensure that the children understand both tests before starting, and give them exactly one minute to complete each test. Be sensitive to those who may require assistance. The children should call out their scores for everyone to record on the database.

Developing Numeracy Handling Data Year 5 © A & C Black 2002

Data project: planning

People in our group

- **Your group is going to plan a survey.**
- **Fill in the boxes below. You must all agree on what to survey.**

Favourite film?

What we plan to survey (think carefully about what you are hoping to find out, and whether people will want to tell you that information)
What resources we will need
What we think the results of the survey are likely to be

- **Now you are going to write a recording sheet for your survey. You could also write a questionnaire.**

Checklist ✓

Think carefully about your questions.
- Could people misunderstand them?
- What are the possible answers?
- Do you need to suggest possible answers for people to choose from?

Think carefully about your recording sheet.
- Is there enough space to record the information?
- How quick will it be to fill in? Can you make it quicker?
- Can you allow extra space for writing any interesting comments?

Teachers' note Use this with pages 41 and 42. Discuss this planning sheet with the class before organising the children into groups. Ensure that the children understand what is required, and suggest different ways in which they could work, distribute responsibility within the group, and record and present the information. Discuss the differences between a recording sheet and a questionnaire.

**Developing Numeracy
Handling Data Year 5**
© A & C Black 2002

Data project: questionnaires

Here are two questionnaires.
One is much better
than the other.
• Can you see why?

> Do you eat bread?
>
> Do you like it?
>
> How often do you eat it?
>
> How much do you eat?
>
> Which type of bread do you prefer?
>
> What spread do you put on your bread?

1. Do you like bread?   yes   no
   (If no, stop the survey now.) ☐   ☐

2. Which type of bread do you prefer?
   brown   ☐
   white   ☐
   wholemeal   ☐
   other _____

3. About how often do you eat bread?
   every day   ☐
   a few times a week   ☐
   less than once a week   ☐
   other _____

4. About how many slices of bread do you eat at:
   breakfast? _____
   lunch? _____
   in the evening? _____
   other _____

5. What spread do you put on your bread? butter   ☐
   margarine   ☐
   none   ☐
   other _____

• Give reasons why the second questionnaire is better.
• Find ways to improve the second questionnaire.

Teachers' note This sheet can be used with pages 40 and 42 to help with the children's data project. Discuss the features of the second questionnaire, such as the sentence following question 1, and draw attention to numbering, tick boxes, wording of questions, and so on. Discuss improvements that could still be made. The children could write further questions for this survey and carry it out.

**Developing Numeracy
Handling Data Year 5
© A & C Black 2002**

Data project: interpreting

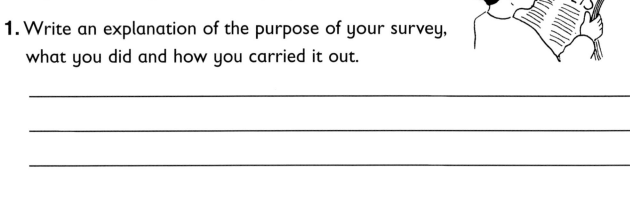

- **Imagine you are reporting the results of your survey in a newspaper.**

1. Write an explanation of the purpose of your survey, what you did and how you carried it out.

_____

_____

_____

_____

2. Now write about your findings. Use some of these words and phrases to write statements about the information you gathered.

most popular	how many less?
most common	same number as
favourite	half as many as
mode	twice as many as
least popular	large difference
least common	small difference
how many more?	range

_____

_____

_____

_____

3. Did the results of your survey turn out the way you expected?   yes ☐   no ☐

4. What was the most unexpected part of the survey?

_____

5. If you were to do this survey again, what would you change?

_____

_____

Teachers' note This sheet can be used with pages 40 and 41 or following any survey that the children have carried out. The children could also present their findings in other ways, for example, as a script for a television documentary or as an interview in which one child plays the role of the interviewer and asks appropriate questions.

**Developing Numeracy
Handling Data Year 5
© A & C Black 2002**

Blank probability scales

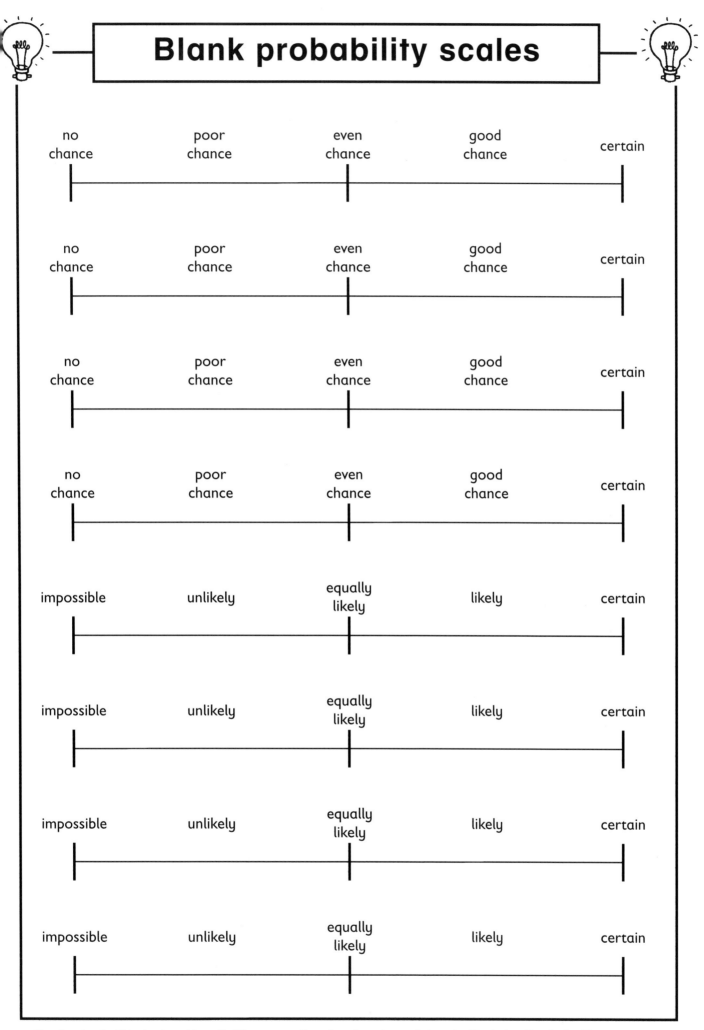

| no chance | poor chance | even chance | good chance | certain |

| no chance | poor chance | even chance | good chance | certain |

| no chance | poor chance | even chance | good chance | certain |

| no chance | poor chance | even chance | good chance | certain |

| impossible | unlikely | equally likely | likely | certain |

| impossible | unlikely | equally likely | likely | certain |

| impossible | unlikely | equally likely | likely | certain |

| impossible | unlikely | equally likely | likely | certain |

Teachers' note This sheet provides a flexible resource. It can be enlarged on a photocopier. The last four scales can be used where there are two equally likely possibilities, for example, when tossing a fair coin.

Developing Numeracy
Handling Data Year 5
© A & C Black 2002

Blank database

Teachers' note This sheet provides a flexible resource which the children can use to create their own databases.

**Developing Numeracy
Handling Data Year 5
© A & C Black 2002**

Blank bar chart

A bar chart to show _____

_____

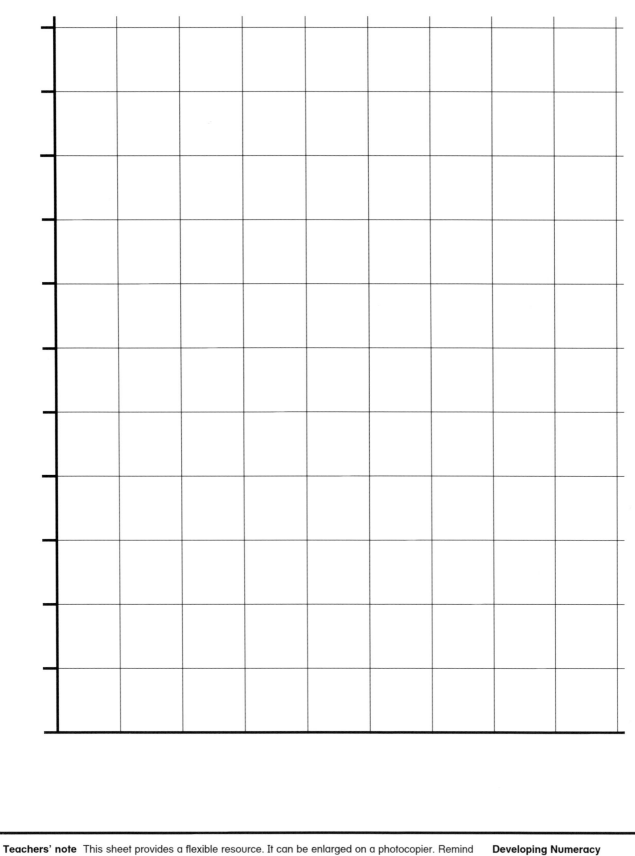

Teachers' note This sheet provides a flexible resource. It can be enlarged on a photocopier. Remind the children of the importance of labelling the axes and giving the chart a title.

Developing Numeracy
Handling Data Year 5
© A & C Black 2002

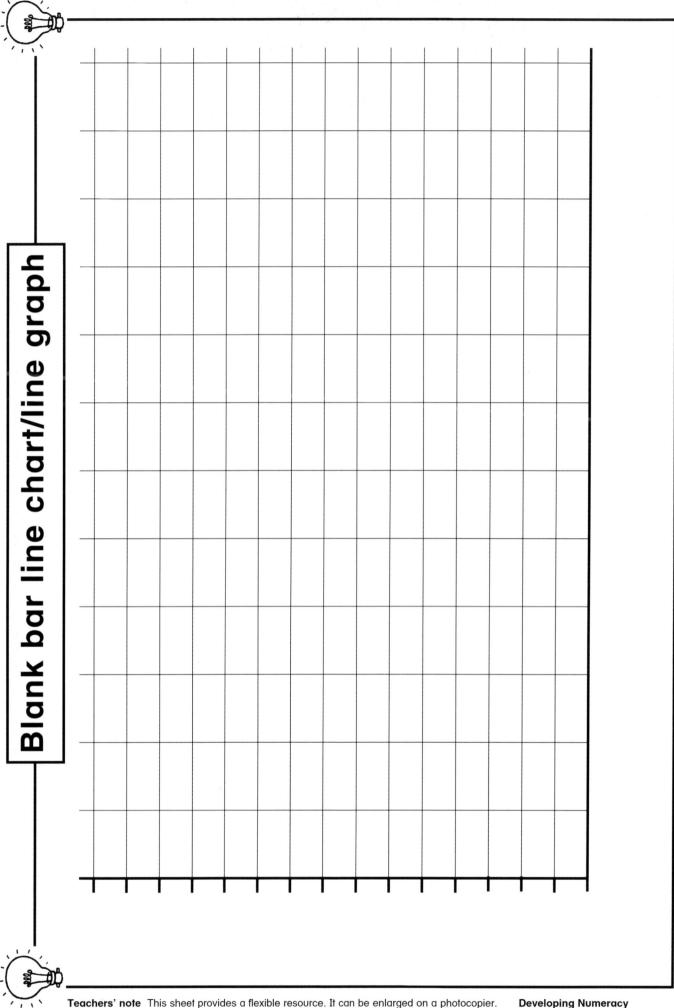

Blank bar line chart/line graph

Teachers' note This sheet provides a flexible resource. It can be enlarged on a photocopier. Remind the children of the importance of labelling the axes and giving the chart a title.

Developing Numeracy
Handling Data Year 5
© A & C Black 2002

Answers

p 10
Now try this!
It would not make any difference if the 6 were changed to a 5.

p 11
Now try this!
The bag contains 1 red sweet, 5 blue sweets and 6 yellow sweets.

p 12
1. Less likely
2. More likely
3. Less likely
4. About as likely
5. More likely
6. About as likely
7. About as likely

p 14
1. 22
2. 15
3. 7

p 15

lighter	3
white	5
toothpaste	2
makes	2
teeth	2
clean	1
and	1
brighter	1

The mode is 'white'.

p 16
4. (a) $2\frac{1}{2}$ hrs
   (b) 5 hrs
   (c) $7\frac{1}{2}$ hrs
   (d) 10 hrs
   (e) $12\frac{1}{2}$ hrs
   (f) 15 hrs

p 17
1. (a) 9   (b) 2
   (c) 0   (d) 1   (e) 5
   (f) 11   (g) 20
   (h) 6   (i) 15
2. 7
3. Check children's answers are reasonable.
4. 3 and 4

p 19

Sally	18	22	Improved by 4
Ben	15	15	No improvement
Urvi	12	17	Improved by 5
Jo	23	27	Improved by 4
Kim	14	19	Improved by 5

p 20
1. (a) 5   (b) 16   (c) 7   (d) 12
2. Noon and 1 pm
3. 7
4. 7
5. Possible, because data is given only for on the hour
6. Between 8 and 9
7. 16

p 21
1. Brachiosaurus 30 m   Pisanosaurus 1 m
   Argentinasaurus 36 m   Diplodocus 27 m
   Tyrannosaurus 12 m   Seismosaurus 45 m
2. Check children's answers.
3. 44 m

p 22
1. (a) 26 g   (b) 31 g
2. (a) baked beans   (b) crisps
3. (a) 4   (b) 8 g
4. (a) 8 bags   (b) 11 bags

p 23
1. (a) 0
   (b) 10   (c) 30
   (d) About 34   (e) About 12
   (f) 5   (g) 5
2. 11 am and noon
3. Check children's answers are reasonable.
4. The machine was refilled.
5. and 6. Check children's answers are reasonable.

p 24
1. (a) 195
   (b) 265   (c) 210   (d) 0
   (e) 150   (f) 332   (g) 167
2. (a) 332 miles
   (b) Saturday
3. Thursday
4. (a) 15
   (b) 98
5. 1319 miles

p 25
1. (a) 8th   (b) 5th   (c) 1st
2. (a) 16 March   (b) 4 May   (c) 6 April
3. 6
4. 5
5. 5
Now try this!
6 April

p 26
1. (a) 2·5 m   (b) 3 m   (c) About 3·3 m   (d) About 3·7 m
2. (a) 2·5 m   (b) About 2·6 m   (c) About 2·7 m   (d) 3 m
3. 50
4. Between 0 and 10 years

p 27

Week 1	Week 2	Week 3	Week 4
true	don't know	don't know	true
true	false	false	true
true	true	false	false
false	true	true	false

Now try this!
Both scales begin at zero.

p 28
1. (a) December   (b) June
2. August
3. (a) 3   (b) 7
4. Between February and March, and between September and October

p 29
1. Check children's descriptions.
2. (a) December   (b) Sun is lower in the sky
3. (a) June   (b) Sun is higher in the sky
4. (a) 5   (b) 5

p 31
1. 11:00 am
2. 2 hours
3. 3 hours
4. About 2:45 pm
5. About 30 minutes
6. At the bank
7. 1 hour
8. About 40 minutes
9. 14 km
10. 9 hours
Now try this!
32 km

p 32
1. July
2. 9 °C
3. 1 °C
4. September
5. December to March
6. July and August

p 33
1. (a) 200 °C   (b) Noon and 1 pm
2. (a) 11:45 am and 5:45 pm   (b) 1 pm and 7 pm
3. $2\frac{1}{2}$ hours
4. 1 pm and 7 pm
5. Door was opened and cold food was put into hot oven.
6. Check children's stories.
Now try this!
About 4 hours

p 34
1. (a) 200 °C   (b) 160 °C
   (c) 110 °C   (d) 20 °C
2. (a) 90 °C   (b) 200 °C
   (c) 160 °C   (d) 120 °C
3. (a) About 1 hour 30 minutes
   (b) About 3 hours 30 minutes
4. (a) About noon and 1:15 pm
   (b) About 11:50 am, 2:30 pm, 5:50 pm and 8:30 pm
5. Check children's stories.
Now try this!
Between noon and 1 pm, and between 6 pm and 7 pm.
Check explanations.

p 35
1. (a) 39 °C
   (b) 8 am Wednesday
2. (a) 36 °C
   (b) 8 pm Friday
3. (a) 38·5 °C
   (b) 37·5 °C
   (c) 37·5 °C
   (d) 38·5 °C
4. (a) 1·5 °C
   (b) 1 °C
5. (a) 1 °C
   (b) 1·5 °C
Now try this!
About 12 hours

p 36
1. a
2. c
3. e
4. f
5. b

p 37
1. (a) 2
   (b) 2
   (c) 5
   (d) 3
   (e) 7
   (f) 1
2. (a) Hannah Harrison
   (b) William Herbert
   (c) Mary Stevenson

p 39
Answers to test 2:
15	30	23	30
16	21	29	37
35	39	40	42
47	43	43	43